# TO BOYS
# UNKNOWN

Because J. Alfred
wasn't singing and
I was a little late,

love

*kx.*

GAY VERSE

# TO BOYS UNKNOWN

*poems by*

## Rev. E. E. Bradford

**Introduced &
Selected by
Paul Webb**

This collection first published 1988 by GMP Publishers Ltd
© Rev. E. E. Bradford
© Routledge & Kegan Paul
Introduction World Copyright © 1988 Paul Webb


**British Library Cataloguing in Publication Data**

Bradford, E.E.
        To boys unknown.
        I. Title
        821'.912

        ISBN 0-85449-092-2


Distributed in North America by
Alyson Publications Inc.,
40 Plympton Street, Boston, MA 02118, USA
telephone: (617) 542 5679

Printed and bound in the EC by Nørhaven A/S, Viborg, Denmark

## Reverend Edwin Emmanuel Bradford

Born 1860. Exeter College, Oxford: B.A. 1884, M.A. 1901, B.D. 1904, D.D. 1912. Curate at High Ongar 1884-6, Walthamstow 1886-7, the English Church at St Petersburg 1887-9, the English Church at Paris 1890-99, Eton 1899-1905. Vicar of Nordelph, Norfolk 1905-44.

## Publications, volumes of verse:

Sonnets, Songs and Ballads, 1908
Passing the Love of Women, 1913
In Quest of Love, 1914
Lays of Love and Life, 1916
The New Chivalry, 1918
The Romance of Youth, 1920
Ralph Rawdon, 1922
The True Aristocracy, 1925
The Kingdom Within You, 1927
Strangers and Pilgrims, 1929
Boyhood, 1930

# Contents

## Introduction

The Reverend Edwin Emmanuel Bradford, a small, sparkling-eyed clergyman, was widely travelled, well read and intelligent. Although he was vicar of Nordelph, in Norfolk, from 1905 to 1944, he had enjoyed many years as a curate overseas, first in St Petersburg, then in Paris. He wrote stories for the immensely popular *Boys' Own Paper*, and published a set of tales about gallant little chaps at the main public schools of England, as well as a collection of sermons which expressed his commonsense insight into the human character and humility. Nothing, one would think, out of the ordinary.

Bradford was however, part of a movement of gay poets which flourished in the forty or so years between the 1890s and the 1930s. In today's atmosphere of AIDS-induced homophobia, with a church tolerant of virtually anything except homosexual priests, it is extraordinary to realise that Bradford churned out openly and cheerfully gay verse from 1908 to 1930. Not only did he think that male love was an alternative to the heterosexual norm, he considered it to be better and more moral, and said so!

His poems range from the cheerful Edwardian charm of a style that can, perhaps, be described as Hinge & Brackett meet John Betjeman, through sensuous poems that correspond to the languid, sun-drenched style of the painter Henry Scott Tuke, to openly sexual affirmations of male love and desire. Betjeman was a friend and an admirer, as was W. H. Auden, who mentions him, in passing, in his poem 'Letter to Lord Byron'. Bradford's poems were immensely popular, and not just among a gay clique. They were reviewed by a huge number of 'respectable' newspapers and journals, including the *Times*, the *Tablet*, and the *Evening Standard*. Some typical comments were:

> He has a verve and a brisk robustness that carry us along with him unprotesting, even if at times somewhat out of breath' (*Literary World*).

> Dr Bradford has gained considerable credit as a writer of easy flowing musical verse, which in many parts convey a deeper philosophy than a casual reader would at first glean from them' (*Belfast News Letter*).

This reaction seems astonishing today. Weren't the 1920s more 'moral' than now? Didn't the papers jump at stories of 'naughty vicars' as much as they do in the 1980s? Was there not censorship of books and paintings, plays and poetry? It is hard to imagine that anyone could be left in doubt of Bradford's message, with poems boasting titles like 'To Boys Unknown', 'The Woodman's Boy', 'The Chorister', 'Free Love', 'I Saw Will Home One Windy Night', and 'Piccadilly'. The poems themselves leave nothing to the imagination, as is shown by 'Piccadilly':

> Loitering in Piccadilly, looking at the shops,
> What should I see but a vision of Apollo...

or 'Fomes Peccati':

> Close by his side a lusty lad lay prone,
> With brawny back, broad loins and swelling
> thighs...

or 'Alan':

> Fresh from his bath, the boy, with hollowed
> hands,
> Luxuriating in the genial heat...

Even if the professional reviewers were all queens it is amazing, first that they recommended his poems to their readers, and second, that the general public lapped then up and begged for more!

Bradford's fame was *not* notoriety. In the *Shell Guide to Norfolk*, produced in the 1950s, Bradford was still mentioned as vicar of Nordelph and literary figure – 'the poet of romantic friendship'. He remained a respected and popular parish priest and was never, as far as one can tell, cautioned by the church authorities. Indeed, had they opposed his open promotion of a gay lifestyle he would not have been able to carry on as a parish priest over four decades.

There are a number of reasons that one can put forward for the failure of the British public (never slow to attack anyone suspected of deviating from staid normality, having leched over the details first) to attack Bradford. First, of course, is the old saying about there being none so blind as those who will not see. If people took his poetry to represent a platonic love between man and boy, of a temporary and helpful nature – such as a scoutmaster might enjoy with his charges – then the poems must have appeared delightfully straightforward or, as the *Times* put it, 'cheery and wholesome'. Second, it *was*, in public at least, a more sexually 'innocent' age than our own, and sex played a less important role in most people's thoughts than is the case with the permissive society generation and their descendants. However, there must have been plenty of gay men who were delighted to read the poems and took full advantage of the public acceptance of Bradford to stock up with his numerous volumes. A major difference between those days and our own was the prevalence then of esteem for a classical education, which gave a certain air of scholarship and respect to aspects of homosexuality – so long as it was expressed in the rarified world of poetry, rather than in the 'real world'.

Whatever the reasons for the acceptance of Bradford's brazenly gay verse, he was able to continue to write, and publish, poems that convey his catching enthusiasms down the many years that separate us from him. We share with him his love of the sea, of blazing heat on firm young bodies which plunge into cool waters and emerge glistening like mermen. We fret with him before he makes a shy offer of affection, and share his joy when he discovers that his love is reciprocated. We follow him on moonlit assignations, don our boaters for picnics on the beach, and live – in our imaginations – in a world where the most passionate feelings are expressed by meaningful looks over the Earl Grey and Bath Olivers.

It is this ability to reach out to us that makes Bradford so likeable a character, and which gives his poetry more depth than just a collection of amusingly camp pieces that would liven up any dinner party. Although his style seems quaint, and very Edwardian (which is, after all, much of its charm), it is infused with a truth, a humanity, and above all, a sense of cheerfulness despite life's setbacks, which endears that small, sprightly vicar to us in our own, very different, lives and times. Speaking of the 'Heat of Love', Bradford wrote:

> When Saints each other see
> With Chaste desire,
> Hell will be verily
> Less hot than heaven!

Let us hope that Dr Bradford, even as we read, is taking tea with the angels.

Paul I. Webb
London 1988

## AT LAST

Returning from Church on a fine June night,
With a shy little fellow called Merrivale White,
I was never so startled in all my life –
   The boy seemed altered quite !

Was it the magic of the woodland way,
The moon, or the scent of the new-mown hay ?
I have no idea: but the fact remains –
   He seemed quite changed that day.

"Look here," he began, "you are going again,
And all this visit I've waited in vain.
Are we going to be chums ? You know what I mean –
   Real mates ? Put me out of my pain."

"But White," I demurred, "you seemed such a kid:
I like you of course, and I always did.
But all I can say is – if you liked me
   You kept it jolly well hid!"

"Did I ?" said he. "Do you mean that you doubted
My feeling for you ?" Then he frowned and pouted.
"Do you think that a boy can offer a man
   His love – and perhaps be scouted ?"

"Do you think that a boy – and a shy boy too –
Finds it easy to come to a man like you,
And propose to be friends – real mates for life ?
   You make a mistake if you do!"

"But I've done it at last." And there his voice broke;
And he lashed at the weeds with his stick as he
   spoke.
Then he went on fiercely, "Whatever you do,
   Don't treat what I say as a joke."

What *I* said or did doesn't matter a straw:
I could see there was no great need to jaw.
I suppose we behaved like a couple of fools –
   But nobody heard or saw.

I only know we were awfully late.
White's father and mother were quite in a state
Till the boy came out with a cock-and-bull tale
   That we couldn't unfasten a gate!

I shall never forget that night in June,
When the scent of the hay, or the gleam of the moon
Made a shy boy bold to break the ice –
   After all it was none too soon!

## THE KISS

### I

He had never done it to Geoff, or to Guy,
  Nor to Arthur – not one of the three:
And I thought that he never would, he was so shy!
  But he did it – he did it to me !

### II

We were out on the beach, and the tide was high,
  And the sun had set over the sea,
And the light was beginning to fade in the sky,
  When I said "You have never kissed me!"

### III

I said it abruptly, I hardly knew why,
  But I said it impetuously;
For it seemed very hard to be bidding "goodbye"
  When my laddie had never kissed me!

*IV*

For a moment he flushed, and fell back with a sigh;
  For a moment he paused doubtfully;
For a moment I feared he was going to cry!
  For a moment I thought he would flee.

*V*

He had never done it to Geoff, or to Guy,
  Nor to Arthur – not one of the three:
But at last, as the day was beginning to die,
  He did it – he did it to me !

## TOO DEEP FOR WORDS

The sun lay low in the Western skies,
  And gilded the Western sea.
"Eric," I said, "'tis a year and a day
  Since first you came to me.
I remember that time so well – do you?"
  "You bet I do!" said he,
"And the crab, and the beautiful Banbury buns
  That we had on the beach for tea!"

While a boy is a boy, he is far too wise
  To paint the pure lily,
Or gild refined gold. That day
  Was full of poetry.
*That* could never be put into word he knew:
  Can the highest ever be?
And surface sentimental talk
  Seemed sheer profanity.

So he just looked up with the love-lit eyes
  That he seldom let me see,
And then, as I pressed the hand that lay
  In mine confidingly,
With a shy little laugh, and a bright flush too,
  "you bet I do!" said he,
"And the crab, and the beautiful Banbury buns
  That we had on the beach for tea!"

## THE CALL

Eros is up and away, away!
Eros is up and away!
The son of Urania born of the sea,
The lover of lads and liberty.
Strong, self-controlled, erect and free,
He is marching along to-day!

He is calling aloud to the men, the men!
He is calling aloud to the men –
"Turn away from the wench, with her powder and
   paint,
And follow the Boy, who is fair as a saint:"
And the heart of the lover, long fevered and faint,
Beats bravely and boldly again.

He is whispering low to the boys, the boys!
He is whispering low to the boys –
"Turn away from the maids of the Evening Star:
My mirrors will show you are prettier far!"
And the rogues are beginning to reckon they are,
And are buying his mirrors for toys!

Aphrodite Pandemos beware, beware!
Aphrodite Pandemos beware!
Go get thee a tunic to cover thy throat,
Or ask Charity sweet for the loan of her coat:
Put a bit and a bridle, I pray, on thy goat,
And bind with a filet thy hair.

But Urania fair be glad, be glad!
Urania fair be glad!
The Goddess of Marriage has nothing to fear:
And to many a man, who would never draw near
Her fortified fane, is the Mother now dear
For the sake of her glorious Lad !

# FRANK

### I

What led him to lay
  His whole heart bare,
When nothing compelled him to?
  Looking away
With a vacant stare,
He dragged all out to view!

### II

There lay a frail
  Bark, launched on life,
At grips with beast and devil:
  Now his artless tale
Would cut like a knife,
Now dance in a witches' revel!

### III

Talk of a fair
  Unveiling her form
To a lover! — What's that to this?
  This boy laid bare
His soul to the storm –
Not his skin to a lover's kiss.

## IV

Well, he has his reward;
  He has won his prize;
(What he sought – be it rich or poor!)
    Truth touched the chord –
And my heart replies,
And will echoe till life be o'er!

## AT THE FAIR

"Where are the whirligigs? Where are the
whirligigs?"
Clamour a chorus of chattering curly-wigs.
  Where? They are everywhere – braying aloud!
Here is a fairing-stand covered with trifles, and
  Here you may shoot for superlative pots.
Crack! Crack! rattle the rifles and
  Bang! Bang! re-echo the shots.
  Eric and I are alone in the crowd.

Showmen who cry at us, roughs growing riotous,
Pushing and pulling us, serve but to quiet us.
  "Look at the moon, Eric, lighting the cloud!
Hark! Do you hear the sea?" Still as a nunnery,
  Peaceful and pure, are Love's sanctified spots.
Crack! Crack! goes on the gunnery,
  Bang! Bang! re-echo the shots,
  But Eric and I are alone in the crowd.

## PICCADILLY

Loitering in Piccadilly, looking at the shops,
What should I see but a vision of Apollo –
Just at the corner where Piccadilly stops,
  Passing into Piccadilly Circus.

Looking at a lithograph led up to a talk –
*He* says that *I* began, *I* say that *he* did!
Anyhow, presently we took a little walk –
  No one introduced us – nobody was needed.

Everybody praises Piccadilly shops:
Piccadilly picture shops beat all the others hollow,
Especially the picture shop where Piccadilly stops,
  Passing into Piccadilly Circus.

# I SAW WILL HOME ONE WINDY NIGHT

## I

I saw Will home one windy night.
  (O how the blast did blow!)
I held his hand, and gripped it tight,
  The storm was raging so.
The ground was white
  With driven snow,
But Love can warm like wine,
  And heat and light
  Both seemed to flow
From the hand I held in mine!

## II

Ere he was home, Will tripped and fell.
  (O how my heart did beat!)
His ankle, sprained, began to swell,
  And the wind grew wet with sleet.
A burden sweet,
  O'er hill and dell,
I bore him after this:
  But aching feet
  And arms grew well
When he paid me with a kiss!

## THE BATHER IN THE BLUE GROTTO AT CAPRI

Prepared to dive, he flings aside his vest,
And waits the signal.  Brown's his curly hair,
Deep brown his eyes, and now we see it bare,
Though face and hands are browner than the rest,
Save two brown nipples on his boyish breast,
His sun-burnt body's nut brown everywhere.
He stands a moment, lit up by the glare
Of light reflected, grave and self-possessed.
Then down he drops deep in the deep-blue wave,
And re-appears a merman.  Silvery scales
Gleam on the grey-blue skin that covers him.
Henceforth he is a creature of the cave –
A fish with human head, and two long tails;
A mythologic monster, sleek and slim.

## SUMMER HEAT

What little breeze there is comes from the South,
  And though in coming it has crossed the sea,
'Tis like a breath from summer's fiery mouth,
  And even hotter than still air can be:
It brought some clouds, but only two or three
  High in the shimmering heav'n can now be seen:
The rest the noonday heat's intensity
  Dissolved in floating haze of glistening sheen,
That forms a lace-like veil with deepest blue
  between.

The tide is high and almost at the turn;
  The fringe of weeds beyond is blanched and dry;
The sands are red, and seem to glow and burn;
  And on the belt of common land hard by
The turf that rabbits nibble on the sly
  Is parched and brown.  Across it beaten tracks
Have formed a path, and here you may descry
  Some beetles creeping out of sun-burnt cracks,
With graceful, slender legs, and green and golden
  backs.

'Tis very still, for almost every bird
    Is put to silence by the blinding heat,
The yellowhammer's call alone is heard,
    Persistent and monotonously sweet,
In yonder fir, the squirrel's rustling feet
    Betray its presence to a practised ear:
And on the ground below, the field-mouse fleet
    Running amid the herbage brown and sere,
Utters from time to time his feeble note but clear.

One human creature – or is it a faun?
    Nay, 'tis a gypsy boy – alone is there.
If he has bathed at all, he has withdrawn
    To bask upon the turf.  His mop of hair
Is dry, and though his lean brown form is bare,
    It shows no sign of damp from head to feet.
His light-contracted pupils boldly stare
    Right at the sun, and seem to find it sweet:
He reigns alone 'mid brutes the genius of the heat.

## MAY FLOWERS

Deep in a sheltered nook; mid hawthorn trees
Laden with snowy blossoms, on the grass,
A lusty ploughboy flung himself at ease,
Close to a pool, whose waters seemed of glass.
As, one by one, his russet rags he doffed,
And let them drop like dead leaves to the earth,
He showed a glowing form, as fair and soft
As is the tender infant's at its birth:
And when, at length, he stood in naked pride,
A boy in beauty, but a man in might,
He put to shame the blossoms at his side,
As sanguine Dawn blots out anaemic Night;
   No other bloom seemed half so sweet and fresh
   As this majestic flower of the flesh!

# FOMES PECCATI

A salt sea-breeze was sweeping in to land
  O'er sandy flames aflame with fiery heat:
But 'mid the shelving store along the strand
  Ran out one weed-strewn rock that stooped to
  greet
    The boist'rous billows foaming at his feet,
Whereat his clammy coat of viscid wrack
  Grew soft and sleek 'neath their cool kisses sweet:
And where the waves welled up above his back
It showed all shifting shades – puce, purple, brown
  and black.

A bright-haired boy with beryl-coloured eyes
  Lay half-reclined thereon and half afloat,
And as he felt the welcome waters rise,
  Soon sweeping swiftly up o'er breast and throat,
    Lifting his body lightly as a boat,
Then sinking till his slender naked form
  Lay bleak and bare, blithe as a wild bird's note
Rang out his happy laughter o'er the storm,
As now he bathed in spray, now basked in sunlight
  warm.

Close by his side a lusty lad lay prone,
  With brawny back, broad loins and swelling thighs
All dimpled o'er with muscle, thew and bone:
  His curly head half-raised was turned slantwise
    Propt on one arm, to let his thoughtful eyes
Drink in the radiant beauty of the boy
  Who, though his gaze was fixed upon the skies,
Perceived and thrilled with shy and modest joy –
The bliss of friendship pure – a bliss without alloy.

And I who passed, with well-approving eye
  In silence watched: then wending on my way
By chance I lighted in a cove near by
  On two young maidens merrily at play.
    Barefoot they paddled in a sheltered bay
Beneath a beetling cliff – a pleasant place
  Secure from prying eyes. One little fay,
The younger, had a sweetly serious face,
And all her slender form breathed purity and grace.

The elder child, she might be twelve or more,
  Was cast in coarser clay.  Both seemed to be
The poorest of the poor: the rags they wore
  Could scarcely veil their nakedness: yet free
    As birds of air, and full of girlish glee
They chirped and chattered in shrill baby tones
  (Not noting or obvious of me
Reclined at ease behind a heap of stones)
Rich in their youth, and gay as queens upon their
  thrones.

But when the sun sloped slowly tow'rd the West
  The boys who I had seen before came by.
They stopped and stared.  The timid child, dis-
tressed,
    Flushed as she caught the elder youth's dark eye
      Fixed on her own. The taller lass, less shy,
Leered at the lad; who, troubled in his turn,
  Blushed hotly; yet half-impudent, half-sly,
Strove with an air of manly unconcern
To meet her bold black, eyes, that seemed to glow
  and burn.

And now the youth came closer to the child
    Scanning her form with studied insolence:
Her sunny face, before so sweet and mild,
    Soon clouded o'er as shadowed by a sense
        Of something undefined. His gaze intense
Pierced through her rags, and where her tattered
    dress
    Yawned wide and left her breast without defence
He gloated on its beauty – none the less
Because he saw her shame and maidenly distress.

Had she been free, for sure she would have fled:
    She whispered to her mate, but all in vain:
The flaunting queen guffawed and tossed her head –
    Her wanton wiles soon made her purpose plain –
        To woo her wished-for wooer. Yet again
The dark youth drew a little nearer. Long
    He bent his eyes full on the child. Her pain
Was almost physical, when sweet and strong
Tolled out a deep church bell for daily evensong.

The lads looked on each other, shamed and shy,
   Then turned with mute consent to climb the hill;
And as I followed where the spire on high
    Pointed to Heaven through the twilight still,
     I pondered on that perfect life where will
Be neither sex nor marriage, and where Love,
    Having no carnal office to fulfil,
Will soar aloft on pinions of the dove,
Leaving his lower half, to seek his spouse above.

# TAKE IT, LAD, OR LEAVE IT!

Here's a loyal and a loving heart,
Take it, lad, or leave it.
Say the word before we part –
Take it, lad, or leave it.
Hoity toity!  Where's the use
Of playing with me fast and loose?
Kiss – or kick me if you choose.
Take it, lad, or leave it!

All I have is freely yours,
Take it, lad, or leave it.
Love – or turn me out of doors!
Take it, lad, or leave it.
Shilly-shally, yes and no,
Won't win a friend or check a foe.
Hold my heart, or let it go –
Take it , lad, or leave it!

## CUTHBERT

When the sun is on the ripples in the West,
And the breeze blows keen from the sea,
And the fisherlad is waiting for the lass loved best,
Cuthbert comes for me:
Cuthbert, grave and severe;
Cuthbert, silent and shy;
With close-cropped hair, eyes dark and clear,
And forehead broad and high.

The fisherlad is welcome to his lass,
I had rather have my boy-friend far;
And I swim by his side through a sea like glass
Lit by Love's one star:
Cuthbert, ghostly and white;
Cuthbert, a bodiless soul;
Now like the Cherubim bright –
With a glorious head for the whole.

## RUDOLF

Boys have no tongues to tell the love they feel:
  Yet one I know will stammer timid phrases
    When none can overhear:
And as each falt'ring word rings true as steel
  Nor woman's wit nor flatt'rer's fulsome praises
    To me are half as dear!

Boys' lips were never framed for eloquence:
  But one I know makes better use of his
    When none are near to spy!
Protesting speeches may be mere pretence:
  No words can say so much as one shy kiss,
    Nor half so prettily!

Leave women then to vow – and lie! not boys:
  But one of these – who's all the world to me! —
    When no one else is nigh,
Will clasp me round the neck: then all the joys
  His halting tongue could never tell break free
    In one long blissful sigh!

## JOE AND JIM

Are we the creatures of our age –
Mere puppets of a passing day?
Our conduct due to heritage
More than to will? 'Tis hard to say.

Two boys were born in seventeen eighty –
We'll call one Joe, the other Jim.
Joe, like the Age, was dull and weighty;
But Jim quick, restless, dark and slim.

Both boys lived in a seaport town:
No matter where. Joe was the son
Of a rich farmer – a mere clown
Who tippled when his work was done.

Jim's father was an officer,
Well-born, but poor for his position.
His mother – Jim took after her –
A beauty, and a great musician.

Both boys were sent to what was then
Described as an Academy
For youthful sons of gentlemen –
A trifle too pretentiously.

In fact it was a third-rate school,
Where boys were, by the Reverened Grey,
Ill-taught, ill-fed, and as a rule
Left to themselves for half the day.

Joe took to Jim: the stolid, simple,
Shy, rosy lad (then just eleven)
At praise from Jim would flush and dimple,
And feel raised to the seventh heaven.

Jim took to Joe: idealist
In love with tenderness and grace,
He had no power to resist
Joe's fresh, fair, flower-like little face.

As for the Age, Jim was still free
From its contaminating breath,
Its vulgar mediocrity,
Its soulless, humdrum life-in-death.

But then the boy had from his birth
A passion for the sea. His eyes
Were turned from sordid sights on earth
To bounding waves and open skies.

Again, the music of that time
No doubt had influenced his heart:
And this, most strangely, was sublime,
Soaring from Handel to Mozart.

Both boys now loved each other – both
Might well have followed one career;
Jim pleaded hard, but Joe was loath:
Does Joe's freewill at last appear?

Had he, or had he not the chance,
Which he would never have on land
Of soaring up to pure romance,
Love, honour – all that's great and grand?

'Twas on the last night of the half,
The two boys slept alone together:
Jim tried persuasion, coaxing, chaff:
Joe only listened to the weather.

The rain fell down in ceaseless streams,
The gusty wind shook all the house,
The lightning flashed in fitful gleams,
And Joe lay trembling like a mouse.

Surely he must have looked at Jim
When now and then the lightning shone?
If he had only glanced at him
But once, I know he would have gone.

For Jim was beautiful: his eyes
Were bright as stars with pure desire:
The love they showed without disguise
Could not but light an answering fire!

But Joe's eyes were shut. He saw within
The creature comforts of his home:
He heard the thunder's awful din:
He made his choice – he would not come.

I have no heart to tell the story
Of Jim – it touches Joe no more.
He died with Nelson, crowned with glory.
But as for Joe our problem's o'er.

Joe had the one chance of his life
And missed it. Do you really care
To hear he married a rich wife,
Drank hard, grew stout, and died a mayor?

# ERIC

Implacable, unmerciful, fulfilled
   To overflowing with the sap of life,
      A male in ev'ry muscle, ev'ry vein:
Contemptuous of weakness, proud, self-willed,
   And cruel in his ardour for the strife
      That steels his heart to his and others' pain:

Impervious to sickly sentiment;
   Clear-headed though hot-blooded; logical,
      And fain to follow Reason to the end:
Careless of creeds and convenance, content
   To trample under foot conventions all
      So he can slay a foe or serve a friend:

Hard-hearted – yes! hard, but not heartless! Nay,
   Afire with love, pure, passionate intense,
      But love that knows no pity – fierce as hate!
He seems a child of that heroic day
   Ere yet man bowed beneath Experience,
      And followed fettered in the train of Fate!

# ALAN

Fresh from his bath, the boy, with hollowed hands,
   Luxuriating in the genial heat,
Before the glowing hearth a moment stands,
   Flushed with its rosy light from head to feet:
And thus I see him, naked, clean and warm,
   Framed by the uncurtained casement close behind,
Placed in a picture lowering with storm,
   'Mid myriad snowflakes whirling in the wind.
His radiant face, illumined by the fire,
   Gleams out against a dark and troubled sea:
The shore, here dank with snow, there foul with
mire,
   Lies all around his form yet leaves it free:
So is it with his heart – 'mid shame and sin
   Unstained it glows with love's pure light within!

# MY LOVE IS LIKE ALL LOVELY THINGS

What is my love like? Why, all lovely things!
  I see them all in him.  When he is gay
He's – let me think – he's like a lark that sings
  Soaring aloft to heaven: or let us say
    A splendid rainbow: or the clang of bells
    Waking the echoes in secluded dells:
He's like Spring, sunshine, flowers – all lovely things!

When he is sad, still all the loveliest things
  Bring back his face to me – he's like them all!
The woods in winter: lonely shores, where rings
  The Church-going bell, and evening shadows fall;
    Or moors in twilight; or a dying hymn
    Heard in an old Cathedral vast and dim:
The sea; the wind; the night – all lovely things!

Is this too vague – like all the loveliest things –
  You cannot picture him?  No more could you
See what I see, without the light love flings,
  If you behold him in the flesh. I, too,
    Saw little in his face at first. I thought
    'Twas fair, but stood alone. 'Twas Love who
    taught
He whom I love was like all lovely things!

## TO BOYS UNKNOWN

How often as I drift along the stream
Of city traffic, till the hive-like hum
Lulls me to sleep, and drowsily I dream
Of sweet days past, or sweeter days to come,
Some boy's fair face breaks on me like a gleam
Of rift-cloud sun, no sooner come than gone.
What if unhailed, unkissed he passes on?
Our hearts have spoken though our tongues were
    dumb.

How often as I ramble on the beach,
Where Nature seems asleep, and man is not,
And fairyland lurks all around, I reach
Some sweet, secluded, world-forsaken spot,
And startle there a shy boy bather. Each
Regards the other doubtful. Suddenly
O'ermastered by some secret sympathy,
Each hails a friend, and doubts are all forgot.

These sweet encounters smack not of our earth:
These mystic boys, met once and never seen
In this life more, scarce seem of human birth.
Henceforth, illum'd by Fancy's golden sheen,
They haunt for ever poppied fields of mirth
Far from our workday world. The fairy Prince,
Mine for a honey'd hour, but vanished since,
Ranks with dream creatures that have never been.

The boys I know and love, though dearer far,
Have faults and failings. These fair friends unknown
Are Visions of Perfection. Naught can mar
The splendour of their memory. Alone
Immaculate, they stand before the bar
Of frowning Justice fearless. Sad-eyed Truth
Knows naught of them; and their immortal youth
No ravages of Time will ever own.

## SONG: "TRAMP, TRAMP, DOWN THE STREET"

Tramp, tramp, down the street
Soldiers march with rhythmic beat;
And tramp, tramp come the pattering feet
Of the children around and behind them.

And a boy I love I shall see to-day –
And maybe see no more! —
Tramp proudly past and march away
To fight on a foreign shore.

Tramp, tramp, every day
Soldiers come and march away:
Tramp, tramp, brave and gay,
While the rattling drums and trumpets play:
Tramp, tramp – but who can say
Where we again shall find them?

## LOVE'S UNREASON

"I'm fond of Joe, it's odd I know,
I never thought I could be.
And though I know I'm fond of Joe
I don't know why I should be."

"He's pretty?" "O dear no,
No prettier than others."
"He's clever?" "May be so,
But no more than his brothers."

"He has some failings." "Oh!
Has he? Then I don't know them."
"And faults." "Indeed! if so
It's certain he don't show them.

"I think I ought to know
If he had few or many.
But faults or failings! Joe?
I'll vow he hasn't any!"

## THE CHOICE

A fair young face, and a clean young heart –
   Thank God, they are neither rare.
You could see that lad was in every part
   As pure as he was fair.

Yet the only boy in a billiard room
   Where one was one too many,
He wore no air of godly gloom,
   But laughed as loud as any.

But when alone, his lips uncurled,
   And brushing away a tear,
He cried, "If these are the ways of the world
   I'll take to your ways – dear."

The "dear" came slyly at the end,
   And made my heart rejoice:
It seemed to sign him as my friend,
   And seal his final choice.

"If these," said he, "are the ways of the world" –
   And his tones rang sharp and clear,
"If these are the ways of men of the world
   I'll take to your ways, dear."

# IN THE DARK

By me, in the motor car,
    Sits a boy – a mere outsider –
Fellow visitor from far,
    For an hour my fellow rider.
        Dark's the night, no moon or star
            Shows his face. Thus flung together,
        English strangers as we are,
            Duly we discuss the weather.
    I hear his voice, I meet his mind,
    But to his body I am blind.

By and by a stray remark
    Touches me: I answer it.
Now what is he saying? Hark!
    That's his heart and not his wit.
        There it lies before me, stark
            Naked, bare, defenceless – mine!
        Love has hit it in the dark,
            Shot it with his shaft divine.
    Heart to heart, and mind to mind,
    Night's good as day since Love is blind!

# DOES DAVIE TELL THE TRUTH?

Davie doesn't care for me,
      So he says.
Couldn't love me – no, not he!
      So he says.
But then he says it with a smile,
In such an enigmatic style,
I can't help wondering all the while
      Does Davie tell the truth?

If he loved, he'd love a lad,
      So he says.
Not a chap as old as dad,
      So he says.
But often after saying this,
He gives me just a little kiss:
So after all the question is
      Does Davie tell the truth?

# THE WOODMAN'S BOY

Deep in the forest beyond the town
I found the woodman's boy:
Ruddy was he, and tanned and brown,
Brimful of life and joy.
Saucy and bold as a woodland elf.
He has made me in love with the woodland itself!
So it's hey for a life in the forest,
That is the life for me!
I want no wealth save youth and health
To roam in the forest free.

When I gave him a kiss he gave me twain,
He was neither sly nor shy.
His laugh was loud, and his speech was plain,
And he looked one straight in the eye.
I have done with maidens timid and pale;
He has made me in love with all things male.
So it's hey for a life in the forest,
Hard toil and manly joy!
I want no wife to smooth my life,
No friend but the woodman's boy.

# THE PRICE OF LOVE

Tired of the rant and fustian of youth,
  And sick of hopes that failed me ere the end,
I cried to Life, "Tell me the sober truth:
  What must I pay, to win and keep a friend?"

Life answered, "First a timely compliment,
  And see that this be generous and sincere;
Then sympathy; then patience, to prevent
  Thy selling cheap the love thou buyest dear.

"These ever: then at times, when comes the call,
  As come it will, for serious sacrifice,
Count well the cost, and if it seem not small,
  Remember love's a treasure of great price.

"But take good heed thy pearl's not counterfeit.
  Assay it; then, if fine, grudge not thy gold.
Sell all thou hast and lay it at Love's feet –
  He will repay it thee a thousandfold."

## NO MISOGYNIST

Men call me a misogynist,
    Women never do:
Women have the wit to see
    'Tisn't true,

Men, of a certain type, insist
    Womankind I hate:
If I hated it would be
    Woman's mate.

Hatred, however, I resist;
    What I may despise,
(Women often there with me
    Sympathise),

Is the complacent sensualist,
    Woman's slave and tool:
Hatred out of place would be
    For a fool.

## SHY LOVE

Little enough say I to Jim,
   Little enough says he,
Though now and again I look at him,
   And he at me:
But if by chance our glances meet –
My faith! I grow as red as beet!

Often I wait for Jim at school,
   Often he waits for me –
With the door between us, as a rule,
   I wait, and he.
When at last he ventures in the street –
Good gracious! how my heart does beat!

"Only a boy," they say of him:
   "Only a boy" is he?
Ay, the only boy in the world is Jim,
   At least for me.
And as for girls, I never meet
One that is fit to kiss his feet!

# THE HEAT OF LOVE

Some say the pure are cold;
  I know they're not:
My love is pure as gold,
  But oh! so warm.
If but his hand I hold
  I straight grow hot:
I burn if I enfold
  His glowing form.

Fire-red's his rosy face:
  But oh! his mouth –
It is the hottest place
  Beneath the sun!
His breath, when we embrace,
  Brings on a drouth
For kisses: in that case
  Ten seem as one!

What wonder this should be
  Since Love is fire,
For is not purity
  Love without leaven?
When Saints each other see
  With chaste desire,
Hell will be verily
Less hot than heaven!

## TO A MOROSE PURITAN

If thou art blind, may not thy neighbour see?
　　If thou art deaf, is he forbid to hear?
If thou art cold, must all men needs agree
　　To banish Love, and harbour Doubt and Fear?
Say thou art straitened and thy lot is drear,
　　Yet wherefore rail at our prosperity?
Say thou art sullen and of evil cheer,
　　Yet why deem mirth and love impurity?
Our bliss is not thy bane; our ill would be
　　No talisman thy clouded heaven to clear.
That thou alone canst do:  I counsel thee
　　To purchase Love, for though the cost be dear,
So to thy cost thou know'st, dear too is hate,
　　And but one grain of love would change thy whole
　　　　estate!

# FREE LOVE

A lover of woman must learn to be
  Content with one, and leave the rest;
But a lover of lads can do like me –
Make love to a hundred equally
  And still love one the best.

I should think it very hard myself
  To have to sit, shut out from heaven,
And hoard my love, as if 'twere pelf,
When I could kiss some roguish elf
  Of let's say six or seven.

And why?  A pretty cause forsooth!
  That fifty miles away or more,
There chanced to be a certain youth
Whose kissing days, to tell the truth,
  Were very nearly o'er!

Would you be jealous, Dick, and pout
  Because I kissed your friends or cousins?
If so, *mon cher*, the truth will out –
  I've kissed young boys in dozens!

## PURITAN PRIDE

Who feel for human love disgust,
   Or shame (save shame more proud than pride)
Would shudder at the sweat and dust
   That fouled and marred the Crucified!

And they who human love distrust,
   And hold its heat unsanctified,
Would coldly sit among the just
   But never kiss the Lamb's sweet Bride.

I had rather have Love marred with lust,
   Blind, jealous, mad, with passion dyed,
Deceitful, cruel, mean, unjust,
   Than purity with scorn allied!

For Love's divine: it may, it must,
   It can, it will be purified!
And Love will live, when "dust to dust"
   Is written on this barren Pride.

## EXCELSIUS

### I

The sweetest thing about boy-love is this –
    Its end is spiritual.
The form's but little, touch embrace and kiss
Are trifles by the way – the prize sought is
    Pure love and mutual.

### II

The woman lover wins the body last,
    And seeks it through the soul;
And last in fact is first in fancy, fast,
And meat's your hope. So, till his race be past,
    The body seems his goal.

### III

We have the form at first, for all we need,
    In its most lovely state:
Our aim's the soul. This must be slowly freed
From boyish flaws, ere we possess indeed
    Our prize – the lifelong mate.

# HIS MOTHER DRINKS

Within a London hospital there lies
> Tucked in his cot,
A child with golden curls and big blue eyes.
> The night is hot,
And though the windows in the long low ward
> Are open wide,
No breath of air comes from the sun-baked yard
> That lies outside.

'Tis Sunday night, and o'er the ceaseless din
> And tramp of feet,
The sound of distant bells comes floating in
> Serene and sweet;
And, by and by, 'mid sighs and smothered groans
> That never cease,
The child's quick ears can catch deep organ tones,
> And hymns of peace.

A kindly nurse who sees his wistful smile,
> To cheer him cries:
"The doctor says that in a little while
> He'll let you rise,
And send you home again!" His eyes grow dim.
> She little thinks
What since his father died home means to him –
> His mother drinks!

The harvest moon flings o'er the gleaming ocean
    A path of gold;
The waves roll in with regular, slow motion;
    While fresh and cold
The breezes blow on pier and beach and crescent;
    Straight in from the sea.
The day was hot and close, but cool and pleasant
    The night will be.

But in a hollow down behind the city
    In courts and slums,
Where most they need the breezes' loving pity,
    No night wind comes.
There in a wretched room, foul and infected,
    A sick child lies,
And helpless, starved, ill-treated and neglected,
    By inches dies.

A fair is on outside – the shouts of showmen,
    Steam organs blare,
And noisy songs of drunken men and women
    Throb through the air.
But in the dark the hapless child is lying,
    And as he sinks,
And bears alone the agony of dying –
    His mother drinks!

## PADDY MALOY

O Paddy Maloy is a broth of a boy,
  As pretty as pretty can be;
He tosses his curls in disdain at the girls,
  For not one is so pretty as he.

Though he's seven years old, he's a bachelor bold,
  As for marrying, simply he won't;
His papa's in despair, for you see he's the heir,
  And the line will run out if he don't.

If a lady but touch him, his anger is such
  That he flushes as red as a rose;
But if he is kissed, in a moment his fist
  Goes simply straight bang at her nose!

What to do with a boy like young Paddy Maloy
  Is a problem to puzzle a sage;
I'm thinking, *ochone!* we must leave him alone,
  For it's too late to change at his age.

## "OUR JACK"

Our Jack's a jolly fisherboy, a sturdy looking chap,
With stubby shocks of curly locks beneath his
battered cap.
His face is tanned and ruddy, and his neck and
throat are brown,
But his skin is like a lady's just a little lower down.
For he's always in the water, and is clean as clean
can be,
And not a baby in the land has fairer skin than he.
There are folks, I know, who grumble and declare *all*
boys are bad,
And when they see one stumble, croak, "A lad *will*
be a lad!"
Of course, we know he will be, but I shouldn't be
afraid
To back a lad that I know against any little maid!
For Jack's always on the water, when the rest are
"on the spree,"
And the parson's little daughter's not more innocent
than he.
Young Charlie's always ready to do his share of
work,
And Freddie, when he's steady, is not the boy to
shirk.
But when the lads get drinking – you may whistle for
them then!

But you'll never find *our* laddie with a lot of
   drunken men.
For Jack, he keeps to water, or at most, a cup of tea,
And there's not a boy in England works more
   heartily than he!

## SKIN-DEEP BEAUTY

### I

'Tis but rarely I stare at luxuriant hair;
  'Tis seldom I think of the skin;
My soul cannot drink of a form that is fair,
  When athirst for the spirit within.
    Dark, light, red, white –
      What does it matter to me?
But if only the spirit be beautiful, all
  To the spirit will beautiful be.

### II

Can I prize or the size or the colour of eyes
  That to honour and duty are blind?
Or is animal beauty enough to disguise
  The lack of a heart or a mind?
    Dark, light, dull, bright –
      What does it matter to me?
If the spirit within be not beautiful, naught
  To the spirit be beautiful be.

# THE PURITY OF YOUTH

A boy makes no parade of holiness,
　　But hides it in his soul's most secret place:
But lest the careless eye should pass it by,
　　God writes it plainly on his radiant face.

His tongue will rarely utter his distress,
　　Keen though it be, at what is foul or base:
God therefore shows his shy, sweet purity
　　In all his slender form's unearthly grace.

Love him, and you will learn his heavenly dress
　　Is sacramental: but in any case
E'en if his form should lie, his modesty
　　Would linger in his kiss and his embrace.

# LOVE AND PASSION

Love comes and goes, as far as Love's mere passion:
Love ebbs and flows, as far as Love's desire;
Anon it glows, in fever's fitful fashion,
   Anon flares out, like fire.

What then? Down underneath, Love in the heart
Laughs at the thunder of the passing storm,
It sees with wonder lightning fires depart,
   And though they die keeps warm.

Spiritual Love dwells in a palace regal
Built far above all paths man's foot has trod.
Meek as a dove , yet stronger than an eagle,
   It soars in rings round God.

## PURE LOVE'S THE BEST

Pure love's the best; no doubt of this:
  'Tis certain, since the Fall,
There's poison in the wanton kiss
  That threatens great and small.

Pure love's the best: the purer 'tis,
  The freer 'tis from gall:
Pure love is everlasting bliss,
  Low pleasures quickly pall.

Pure love's the best: and yet, I wis,
  All own who life recall,
'Tis better to have loved amiss
  Than ne'er have loved at all.

## "WHEN FIRST I FELL IN LOVE WITH YOU"

"When first I fell in love with you – "
"In love with me? In love with me?"
"A prettier boy I never knew,
And never wished to see!"
"But out with it! Come, out with it!
Never mind the first.
What of the present? Tell me true,
It is better to know the worst."

"Why, now you are big and brown and stout – "
"So I'm aware! So I'm aware!"
"A very good chap, I make no doubt – "
"That's neither here nor there.
But out with it! Come, out with it!
So since you saw me first
I've grown into a hulking lout?
Well, it's better to know the worst."

"Since I first fell in love with you,
And you with me, and you with me,
Of prettier boys I've seen a few,
And more I hope to see;
Still – " "Out with it! Come, out with it!
It's better to know the worst."
"I'm ten times more in love with you
Than ever I was at first!"

# WE SHALL ALL LOOK NICE IN HEAVEN

### *I*

My love had  a frail little body,
  And his sweet litle face was plain;
And neither were any the fairer
  When wasted away with pain.
Often, when brushing his hair, I could see
  He would look in the glass rather wistfully.
And the night that he died he whispered to me
  "Shall we all look nice in heaven?"

### *II*

I have borne his frail little body
  On a bare little bier to-day.
The body, the bier, and the bearer
  Were all of a piece you'd say.
Afterward, there in its usual place,
  Hung the glass that he used, and I saw my face!
Well, what does it matter?  In any case
  We shall all look nice in heaven.

## THE CHORISTER

### I

The Church was dark, save round the lighted Altar:
  The air was hot, and heavy with incense.
The Chorister's sweet tones began to falter
  And die away with passion too intense:
"O Paradise, O Paradise, 'Tis weary waiting here,
I want to be where Jesus is, to know and feel Him
  near."

### II

Outside the heath-clad moor was bathed in light;
  A keen sea breeze blew freshly from the West:
The Chorister, no longer robed in white,
  Was boy again, calm, cool, and self-possessed.
"True?  No," he faltered.  "Yet some thought
  behind the words was true:
I longed for something – was it home?  And some
  one – was it you?"

# TRAMPS

I was tramping in the gloaming
When I met with Alec Grey –
Tramping in the gloaming
On a dark, damp day.
But though both of us were tired
And sodden and bemired,
From the moment of our meeting
We grew quite gay.
For each had found in other
One dearer than a brother,
And we laid us down together
In the soft, warm hay.
What's stormy weather,
And what's a little mire,
With a hayrick for a shelter,
And love for fire?

We have tramped it now a lifetime
Alec Grey and I —
Tramped it now a lifetime,
God knows why.
No end to it appears,
And we're getting on in years,
But still we keep on hoping,
And our hearts beat high:
For each has found in other
One dearer than a brother,
And we'll lay us down together
When the end draws nigh.
What's a life of failure,
And what's a death of pain,
As long as we're together
When we wake again?

*Gay Verse from GMP — The Gay Men's Press*

## THE ANGEL OF DEATH IN THE ADONIS LOUNGE
Poems by
Marc Almond
ISBN 0-85449-079-5
80 pages UK £3.95/ US $7.95

## NOT LOVE ALONE
Martin Humphries(ed)
Anthology of gay verse by 30 modérn gay poets
ISBN 0-85449-000-0
144 pages UK £3.50/ US $6.50

## DREAMS AND SPECULATIONS
Poems by
Paul Binding & John Horder
ISBN 0-85449-039-6
64 pages UK £2.95/ US $5.95

**SO LONG DESIRED**
Poems by
James Kirkup & John McRae
ISBN 0-85449-038-8
64 pages UK £2.95/ US $5.95

**THREE NEW YORK POETS**
Poems by
Mark Ameen, Carl Morse & Charles Ortleb
ISBN 0-85449-052-3
96 pages UK £3.95/ US $7.95

**TONGUES UNTIED**
Poems by
Dirg Aaab-Richards, Craig G Harris,
Essex Hemphill, Isaac Jackson &
Assotto Saint
ISBN 0-85449-053-1
96 pages UK £3.95/ US $7.95

GMP books can be ordered from any bookshop in the UK, and from specialised bookshops overseas. If you prefer to order by mail, please send full retail price plus £1.00 for postage and packing to GMP Publishers Ltd (M.O.), PO Box 247, London N15 6RW. (For Access/Eurocard/Mastercharge/American Express give number and signature.) Comprehensive mail-order catalogue also available.

In North America order from Alyson Publications Inc., 40 Plympton St, Boston MA 02118, U S A.

NAME AND ADDRESS IN BLOCK LETTERS PLEASE:

Name .....................................................

Address ...............................................

..............................................................

..............................................................

..............................................................